BARBADOS TRAVEL GUIDE 2024

The updated guide to Barbados history and culture, places to visit, top sight, beaches, lodging options, and hidden gems

CATHY GREG

Copyright © 2024 by Cathy Greg

All rights reserved. No part of this publication may be reproduced, distributed, or transmitted in any form or by any means, including photocopying, recording, or other electronic or mechanical methods, without the prior written permission of the publisher.

CONTENTS

INTRODUCTION.. 5
   Historical Background... 7
   Cultural Significance.. 8

CHAPTER ONE: TRAVEL REQUIREMENTS................ 11
   Best Seasons to Visit... 11
   Considerations for the Weather............................ 11
   Crowds of tourists.. 12
   Cultural and Festive Activities............................... 12
   Requirements for Travel Documentation and Entry.............. 13
   Visas and passports... 13
   Return tickets and proof of lodging...................... 14
   Requirements for Health and Vaccination......... 14
   Allowances for Customs and Duty-Free Shopping................ 14
   Payment Methods and Currency............................ 15

CHAPTER TWO: GETTING TO AND AROUND BARBADOS... 17
   Airport and Air Travel Information....................... 17
   Modes of Public Transportation............................ 19
   Barbados Car Rentals and Driving........................ 21
   Driving on the island of Barbados......................... 22

CHAPTER THREE: ACCOMMODATIONS.................... 24
   Luxury Resorts and Hotels..................................... 24
   The Allure of Barbados' Luxury Accommodations............... 24
   Budget and Mid-Range.. 27
   One-of-a-Kind Accommodations: Villas and Guesthouses... 29
   The best hotels in Barbados.................................... 32

CHAPTER FOUR: ATTRACTIONS AND SIGHTSEEING 45

Beaches and Natural Wonders..45
Historical Monuments and Museums.................................45
Natural Attractions and Parks..46
Cultural and Community Activities....................................47
Top 10 destinations to explore in Barbados.........................48

CHAPTER 5: ACTIVITIES AND EXPERIENCES........... 59
Water Sports and Marine Adventures..................................59
Windsurfing and surfing...59
Snorkeling and Scuba Diving...60
Kayaking and stand-up paddleboarding...............................60
Deep Sea Fishing..61

CHAPTER 6: FOOD AND DINING.................................62
Traditional Bajan Cuisine..62
Fine Dining & International Cuisine:..................................66
Street Food and Fast Food:...67
Fine Dining & International Cuisine:..................................68
Street Food and Fast Food:.. 68

CHAPTER 7: PRACTICAL INFORMATION FOR TRAVELERS..70
Health and Safety Recommendations..................................70
Cultural Etiquette and Customs.. 72
Communication and connectivity..74

CHAPTER 8: DAY TRIPS AND EXCURSIONS................77
Attractions and Islands Nearby... 77

CHAPTER 9.. 83
SUSTAINABLE TOURISM IN BARBADOS................... 83
Environmental Initiatives...83
Participate in Local Communities...................................... 86
Tips for Safe Travel.. 87

CONCLUSION...91

INTRODUCTION

Barbados, a small Caribbean island nation, is a one-of-a-kind blend of breathtaking natural beauty, vibrant culture, and rich history. It is around 430 square kilometers in size and is located in the Atlantic Ocean northeast of Venezuela. The island is generally level, except for a few gently rising hills to the north.

Barbados has a tropical climate with two seasons: wet from June to November and mild from December to May. Its pristine beaches, with crystal blue waves and fine sand, are among the Caribbean's most attractive, attracting visitors worldwide. The west coast is recognized for its calm waters and exquisite resorts, but the east coast, which faces the Atlantic, is noted for its rougher terrain and more giant waves.

Barbados' economy is highly reliant on tourism and offshore banking. The island's political stability, well-developed legal and educational systems, and modern infrastructure make it an appealing business and leisure destination. As a former British colony, it maintains a parliamentary system of government and is a member of the Commonwealth.

Barbados is a cultural melting pot, displaying the influence of African, Indian, Irish, Creole, and British history. Its cuisine, music, dancing, and festivals reflect this diversity. Calypso, reggae, and the indigenous form of spouge are prevalent on the island's music scene.

Barbados is also becoming more environmentally conscious, with initiatives to safeguard its natural resources and mitigate the effects of climate change. The island's coral reefs, sea turtles, and rich marine life are critical to its ecological and economic health.

Barbados is a small yet intriguing Caribbean island noted for its natural beauty, rich cultural legacy, and thriving economy. It is a prime example of a prosperous, varied, sustainable island nation.

Historical Background

Barbados' history includes indigenous, colonial, and post-colonial elements. The Arawak and Carib peoples arrived from South America and were the first to settle on the island. Until the coming of European conquerors, these indigenous populations mainly subsisted by fishing, hunting, and farming.

Spain claimed Barbados in the late 15th century, but the English later established it in 1627. The English constructed sugar plantations, which altered the island's economy and society. Sugar production, fueled by slave labor imported from Africa, enabled Barbados to become one of the world's leading sugar producers by the 18th century.

The slave trade and the plantation system greatly influenced Barbadian civilization. The majority of the population was made up of enslaved Africans. And they were subjected to atrocities. Their perseverance, resistance, and cultural influences are deeply woven into the island's social fabric.

Slavery was abolished in 1834, bringing about significant social changes.

Barbados gradually moved toward self-government in the twentieth century. It became a self-governing colony in 1961, earning complete independence from the United Kingdom in 1966. Since its independence, Barbados has maintained stable democratic governance and established a diverse economy, lessening its reliance on sugar.

Barbados has always played an essential part in Atlantic trade networks and the Caribbean's political and social dynamics. While its colonial history has caused much grief and injustice, it has also contributed to the rich cultural tapestry that defines the island today.

Cultural Significance

Barbados' cultural significance stems from its unique tapestry of African, European, and indigenous influences, which have molded the island's character. Barbadian culture, often known as "Bajan" culture, is reflected in its music, dancing, food, language, and festivals.

Music and dancing are essential parts of Barbadian culture. Calypso and soca music, commonly linked with the lively Crop Over event, originate in the island's African ancestry and colonial past. This festival, which began as a celebration of the conclusion of the sugar cane harvest, has evolved into a bright, exuberant display of Barbadian song, dancing, and costume.

The island's food reflects its cultural melting pot, integrating African, Indian, and British influences. Traditional meals such as cou-cou, flying fish, pudding, and souse are delicious and essential to the island's past and identity.

Barbados' literary and cultural scenes are equally noteworthy, with several Barbadian writers and artists achieving international fame. The island's literary works frequently tackle identity, colonialism, and post-colonialism, reflecting Barbados' complex past and varied cultural terrain.

The official language of Barbados is English. However, Bajan Creole, a variant inspired by West African languages and English, is widely spoken. This language is a monument to the island's history and cultural diversity.

Religion is essential in Barbadian society, with Christianity being the dominant faith. The religious landscape of the island is peppered with old churches, reflecting the island's colonial heritage and the continued relevance of religion in everyday life.

Barbados has various historical landmarks, notably the UNESCO World Heritage-listed Bridgetown and Garrison. These sites serve as memories of the island's colonial history and are critical to comprehending the island's current cultural identity.

Finally, Barbados' cultural relevance is anchored in its history of convergence and persistence. The island is a monument to its people's perseverance and inventiveness, making it more than just a tropical paradise but also a center of a rich cultural legacy.

CHAPTER ONE: TRAVEL REQUIREMENTS

Best Seasons to Visit

Barbados is a year-round attraction due to its mild climate and gorgeous scenery. However, the optimum time to visit is mainly determined by personal choices, such as weather, tourist crowds, and cultural events.

Considerations for the Weather

Barbados has a tropical climate with two distinct seasons: dry and wet. The dry season, which runs from December to May, is considered the best time to visit for people searching for sunny, beach-perfect weather. During this period, the island receives little rain, and temperatures range from 23°C to 31°C (73°F to 88°F). Rainfall and tropical storms or hurricanes are more common during the rainy season, which lasts from June to November. However, rain often falls in quick, heavy showers, followed by sunshine, and does not significantly disrupt travel plans.

Traveling during this period can benefit those looking for fewer tourists and lower prices.

Crowds of tourists

The dry season coincides with Barbados's peak tourist season, which lasts from mid-December to mid-April. This is the peak season for visitors to the island, resulting in crowded beaches and increased prices for lodgings and activities. Consider going between late November and early December or April and early June.

Cultural and Festive Activities

Throughout the year, Barbados conducts various cultural events, providing tourists unique experiences. The most prominent is the Crop Over Festival, a traditional harvest festival that has evolved into a vibrant, all-encompassing celebration of Bajan music, dance, food, and culture. Crop Over, from June to the first Monday in August, culminates with the Grand Kadooment Day, a colorful and exciting street parade.

For sports enthusiasts, the Barbados Surf Pro in April and numerous cricket tournaments throughout the year are worth considering. Furthermore, the Barbados Food and Rum Festival in October and the Barbados Jazz Excursion in early October draw many visitors. To summarize, weather preferences, crowd tolerance, and interest in local events determine the best time to visit Barbados. The dry season gives perfect beach weather, while the wet season offers a more relaxed experience with the possibility of showers.

Requirements for Travel Documentation and Entry

Traveling to Barbados necessitates some planning in terms of paperwork and understanding the admission procedures.

Visas and passports

All visitors to Barbados are required to have a valid passport. Your passport must be good for the entire duration of your visit. For short stays (typically up to 90 days), visitors from numerous countries, including the United States, Canada, the European Union, and several Caribbean states, do not need a visa. However, it is critical to check your nation's most recent visa regulations before flying.

Return tickets and proof of lodging

Upon arrival, travelers may be asked to show proof of return or forward travel and proof of housing. This can include return flight tickets, hotel booking confirmations, or the location where you will stay in Barbados.

Requirements for Health and Vaccination

There are no mandatory immunization requirements for tourists to Barbados. Visitors should, however, have all necessary vaccines. In light of global health challenges such as the COVID-19 pandemic, travelers should review any particular health-related entry criteria or travel advisories before departure.

Allowances for Customs and Duty-Free Shopping

Visitors to Barbados should be aware of customs regulations, particularly duty-free exemptions for items such as alcohol and tobacco. To avoid complications upon arrival, check the most recent laws.

Payment Methods and Currency

Understanding the currency and payment methods is critical for a trouble-free trip to Barbados.

Currency

Barbados' currency is the Barbadian Dollar (BBD), tied to the US Dollar at a fixed rate of about 2 BBD to 1 USD. Although US dollars are frequently accepted throughout the island, Barbadian dollars typically provide change. It's a good idea to bring some local currency with you for little purchases, tips, and situations where US dollars may not be accepted.

ATMs and credit cards

Most hotels, restaurants, and larger retailers accept major credit cards such as Visa and MasterCard. On the other hand, smaller shops, local markets, and rural locations may only get cash. ATMs are commonly available, particularly in urban areas and near tourist attractions, and most of them accept Barbadian and US dollars.

Gratuities and Service Fees

Tipping is prevalent in Barbados, while some places incorporate a service tax (often 10-12.5%) in the bill. A 10-15% tip is usual for services where the information is not included, depending on the quality of service.

Fees and exchange rates

Travelers should know currency conversion rates and associated costs while exchanging money or using credit cards abroad. It is frequently more advantageous to exchange money at a bank or authorized currency exchange shop than at an airport or hotel. Finally, knowing when to visit Barbados, preparing the essential travel papers, and understanding the currency and payment methods can ensure a smooth and enjoyable journey to this lovely Caribbean island.

CHAPTER TWO: GETTING TO AND AROUND BARBADOS

Airport and Air Travel Information

Barbados air travel

Barbados is well-connected by air, principally via Grantley Adams International Airport (GAIA), the island's sole airport at Seawell, Christ Church. This airport is a significant gateway not just to Barbados but also to the Eastern Caribbean.

Routes and major airlines

Several international airlines fly to Barbados from North America, Europe, and other Caribbean islands. Direct flights from major US cities such as New York, Miami, and Fort Lauderdale are available. Direct flights from Canadian cities such as Toronto and Montreal are available. European connections are generally made via London and Manchester in the United Kingdom.

Caribbean Airlines connects Barbados to other Caribbean destinations via regional flights. The frequency and availability of these flights are affected by seasonal changes, with more options available during winter when tourism is at its highest.

Airport Services and Facilities

Grantley Adams International Airport has various facilities and services to meet the needs of travelers. Duty-free shops, cafés, currency exchange services, automobile rental businesses, and tourist information offices are among them. Wi-Fi is also available, as are lounges and facilities for passengers with special needs.

Transfers from the Airport

Taxis, buses, and vehicle rental services are available from GAIA to various island regions. Taxis are widely accessible outside the terminal, with fixed prices to multiple destinations. Public buses serve the airport, giving links to Bridgetown and other significant regions at a lower cost.

Air Travel Preparation

When planning an aviation trip to Barbados, double-check visa requirements and health and safety regulations, especially in light of global events such as the COVID-19 pandemic. Early booking is advised, particularly during peak tourist seasons.

Modes of Public Transportation

Buses

Barbados' public transit is dependable, inexpensive, and a fantastic opportunity to experience local life. The Barbados Transport Board (government-owned) and private operators known as "mini buses" and "ZR vans" (private route taxis) operate the island's bus system.

Buses for the Government

These blue buses, including famous tourist spots, cover most of the island and have set schedules and rates. They operate from the significant Bridgetown terminal as well as various smaller terminals. Buses run at regular intervals, though they are less frequent on Sundays and holidays.

ZR Vans and minibuses

Minibuses (yellow with a blue stripe) and ZR vans (white with a maroon stripe) run more frequently but with less predictability. They are well-known for their upbeat music and energetic atmosphere. These vehicles typically follow major bus routes but can be summoned from anywhere.

Passes and Fares

Bus fares are very affordable, although exact change is frequently required. For frequent bus riders, multi-ride passes might be a practical and cost-effective choice.

Public Transportation Suggestions

Expect a spirited, often cramped ride on mini buses and ZR vans. Keep modest notes and coins on hand for fare payments.

Be aware of your route and stops; buses may only stop at all scheduled visits if instructed.

Barbados Car Rentals and Driving

Car Rental Alternatives

Renting a car allows you to explore Barbados on your own time. In Barbados, there are numerous automobile rental organizations, ranging from worldwide chains to local businesses. Rental cars are at the airport, in Bridgetown, and in popular tourist spots.

Renting Requirements

To rent a car in Barbados, you must first:
- You must be at least 21 (age requirements may vary according to the rental business).
- A valid driver's license from your home country is required.
- Obtain a Barbados driver's license (available via automobile rental companies or local police stations).

Barbados drives on the left side of the road, whereas most rental automobiles are right-hand drive. The island's road network is substantial, with highways connecting significant towns and attractive coastline roads.

Navigation and Road Conditions

While generally in decent shape, secondary roads might be narrow and uneven. Although road signage is adequate, owning a GPS or a map can help you navigate, especially in rural areas. Bridgetown traffic can be crowded, especially around peak hour.

Driving Suggestions

In cities, speed limits are 60 km/h (37 mph) on highways and 20-40 km/h (12-25 mph). Be cautious of pedestrians, bicycles, and the occasional cattle on the road.Bridgetown has parking meters and designated spots for parking.

Alternative Modes of Transportation

Taxis and guided trips are beautiful choices for folks who are uncomfortable driving. Taxis in Barbados do not have meters; thus, it is best to agree on a fare ahead of time. Tours, on the other hand, provide the benefit of guided exploration of the island's main attractions.

Getting to and about Barbados is made more accessible by various options, ranging from convenient air travel to an extensive public transportation network to flexible vehicle rental services. Each method of transportation provides a unique way to enjoy the island, catering to tourists' different interests.

CHAPTER THREE: ACCOMMODATIONS

Luxury Resorts and Hotels

Barbados, a Caribbean treasure, is recognized for its magnificent beaches, vibrant culture, and luxury lodgings. The island's luxury resorts and hotels blend richness, relaxation, and world-class service, making it a popular choice for travelers wanting a high-end vacation experience.

The Allure of Barbados' Luxury Accommodations

Luxury resorts in Barbados are more than simply opulent accommodations and high-end amenities; they offer a comprehensive view of the island's allure. These facilities are frequently strategically positioned to provide spectacular ocean views, exclusive beach access, and an atmosphere of exclusivity and tranquility.

Iconic Luxury Resorts

Sandy Lane: Sandy Lane embodies luxury and elegance. This resort is known for its excellent service and offers luxurious accommodations and suites, a world-renowned spa, and various fine-dining restaurants. Its golf course is a significant draw, providing one of the best golfing experiences in the Caribbean.

Crane Resort: The Crane Resort, perched on a spectacular cliff overlooking one of the world's most stunning beaches, combines old-world elegance with modern luxury. The resort is well-known for its vast apartments, private pools, and breathtakingly magnificent beach.

Coral Reef Club: The Coral Reef Club, a family-owned treasure, is famed for its classic island elegance. Nestled in a lovely garden setting, this hotel offers exquisite accommodations, fine cuisine, and a tranquil spa in a colonial-inspired ambiance.

Exclusive Services & Amenities: Barbados' luxury resorts go above and beyond typical amenities to provide customized services. Personalized butler services, exclusive dinner experiences, and custom excursions are just a few examples. These places frequently offer a variety of dining alternatives, including specialist restaurants run by well-known chefs.

Leisure and Wellness: Many luxury hotels in Barbados are focused on wellness and leisure, with cutting-edge fitness centers, yoga courses, and substantial spa amenities. The spas use local ingredients and practices to provide a one-of-a-kind wellness experience.

Excursions and activities: These resorts frequently provide unique activities and excursions for their guests, ranging from private yacht charters and deep-sea fishing to cultural tours and cookery workshops. Golf enthusiasts will find some of the Caribbean's top golf courses in Barbados, many of which are affiliated with luxury hotels.

Destination Weddings and Events: Barbados is a popular wedding and event destination, with luxury hotels offering stunning settings, bespoke planning services, and gourmet dining. These hotels can make dream weddings a reality, whether it's a seaside ceremony or a big ballroom celebration. Barbados' finest resorts and hotels provide more than simply a place to stay; they offer an entire immersion into the island's culture, natural beauty, and polished elegance. With its distinct charm and superb service, each property ensures a beautiful and enjoyable visit for the discerning tourist.

Budget and Mid-Range

While Barbados is known for its luxurious accommodations, the island also has a variety of cheap and mid-range accommodation alternatives. These lodgings provide affordable comfort, convenient locations, and genuine Bajan hospitality, making Barbados more accessible to guests.

A Wide Range of Low-Cost Accommodations: Budget and mid-range lodgings in Barbados range from beautiful guesthouses and boutique hotels to self-catering apartments and inns.

Bed and Breakfasts: Guesthouses and Bed & Breakfasts provide a more intimate and personalized lodging experience. These places are frequently family-run and create a welcoming atmosphere. They are ideal for those who prefer engaging with locals and other guests.

Boutique Hotels: Boutique hotels mix economical luxury with customized attention. These hotels frequently have distinctive designs that reflect the island's culture and traditions. They may have fewer amenities than luxury resorts but they do not skimp on comfort and pleasure.

Self-Catering Apartments: Self-catering flats are an excellent option for individuals who prefer a more independent type of vacation. These facilities frequently have fully equipped kitchens, allowing guests to cook meals, which can be a substantial cost-saver.

Inns and Low-Cost Hotels: Barbados' inns and cheap hotels provide simple but decent lodging. These are great for visitors who spend most of their time touring and need a simple, clean, and safe place to relax.

Value for money: Barbados' budget and mid-range accommodations provide excellent value. They offer vital amenities such as air conditioning, clean rooms, and, in some cases, Wi-Fi and swimming pools without the high price tag of luxury resorts.

Location and accessibility: Many of these low-cost lodgings are conveniently placed near major beaches, attractions, and local dining options. The proximity to public transportation is particularly advantageous, allowing for easy island exploration.

Experiencing Local Culture: Staying in budget or mid-range lodgings generally affords more opportunity to engage with people and experience the accurate Bajan way of life. Many of these establishments are in residential areas, providing a look into daily life in Barbados. Barbados' budget and mid-range accommodations are ideal for guests seeking value, comfort, and an authentic experience. These solutions ensure that the beauty and charm of Barbados are accessible to everyone, regardless of budget.

One-of-a-Kind Accommodations: Villas and Guesthouses

Barbados has a variety of unique hotel alternatives that allow visitors to experience the island's appeal in a more intimate and personalized setting. Villas and guesthouses are trendy for home-like comfort and local flavor.

Villas: A Touch of Luxury and Privacy Renting a villa in Barbados is a beautiful option for families, parties, or tourists seeking extra solitude and space.

Villa Styles: Barbados villas range from spectacular beachfront residences to more private, garden-surrounded dwellings. They come in various sizes, with amenities ranging from private pools and vast terraces to fully furnished kitchens and on-site staff.

Advantages of Villa Stays: Privacy and Space: Villas provide a private, home-like environment, ideal for people who prefer to avoid the crowds of hotels and resorts.

Cost-Effective for Groups: Villas can be a cost-effective alternative for families or groups, providing more space and facilities for the same or lower price as many hotel rooms.

Flexibility & Freedom: Villas allow you to choose your schedule, cook meals, and relax in a space that feels like home.

Guesthouses: Authenticity and Interaction with Locals Guesthouses in Barbados provide a more authentic overnight experience at a lower cost.

The Allure of Guesthouses: Guesthouses, which are generally family-owned, offer a warm, intimate setting. They provide a glimpse into the Bajan way of life, with hosts frequently prepared to impart local knowledge and, occasionally, home-cooked meals.

The Advantages of a Guesthouse Stay: Cultural Immersion: Staying in a guesthouse provides more interaction with residents and a more direct encounter with the island's culture.

Personalized Service: The smaller scale of guesthouses frequently translates to more personalized care and a familial feel. Guesthouses are typically less expensive than hotels and resorts, making them perfect for budget-conscious guests. Unique Barbados lodgings, such as villas and guesthouses, offer solitude, local flavor, and a more personalized experience. These options appeal to various preferences and budgets, ensuring every visitor can find a comfortable and enjoyable location to stay on the island.

The best hotels in Barbados

Barbados has its own laid-back Caribbean island charm, with lazy afternoons spent on white-sand beaches that drop into dreamlike blue coves, but this coral island is more than sand and sea. Bridgetown, a UNESCO World Heritage site, buzzes with independent shops, markets showcasing Bajan produce and crafts, and historic (typically rum) structures like St Nicolas Abbey. Roadside rum shacks are as typical as tropical gardens – the Andromeda Botanic Gardens near Bathsheba hamlet are particularly gorgeous – and festivals like The Food and Rum Festival and Crop Over Festival offer a glimpse into Bajan culture. For many weeks, street performers in flashy costumes take to the streets; the scent of spiced sweet potatoes, chicken curry, and fried flying fish fills the air.

Barbados, only 21 miles from tip to tip, delivers this blend of beach and culture to all regions - surfers flock to the underappreciated east coast for its Atlantic waves. In contrast, sunbathers flock to the west for the quiet, bath-warm waters of the Caribbean Sea. Although certain portions of the island have succumbed to all-inclusive culture, Barbados' coastlines are home to a slew of chic hotels, many of which harken back to a bygone period of pre-lunch gin and tonics over backgammon, and a few of which channel the island's no-frills ethos with inventive Creole dishes and whitewashed suites.

From family-owned pillared legends with country club rhythms and back garden areas of the perfect beach to pared-down boutiques with Calypso music and dishes of freshly caught seafood, here are the most lavish hotels in Barbados. For more information, see our list of the best all-inclusive Barbados resorts.

Cobbler's Cove:

Aside from the stunning striped pink scalloped umbrellas, this family-owned boutique hotel's trump card is its quarter mile of powder-soft beach in a hidden cove. Pastel-colored rooms are set around tropical gardens covered with palms and banana leaves, and a ceramic pool terrace hangs like a theatrical throne with bay views.

Rooms pour onto terraces framed by bougainvillea, savoring the salty breeze. Camelot and Colleton are the coral-washed Great House's hot-ticket turreted rooms, with rooftop patios and beautiful bay views. The main spaces are laid out like a British country house, complete with a drawing room and a vast hall, but with exotic pinks, greens, and plantation shutters - a mix that symbolizes the island's rich (and often tumultuous) history.

Cobblers Cove's mornings are reminiscent of old-fashioned country clubs, where a sophisticated breakfast noise is occasionally disturbed by the pop of a tennis serve or a

Champagne cork. Sedate afternoons are often spent lounging between sun loungers and the warm sea, where guests can paddle out for turtles or gently split the quiet, clear water on a paddle board. Guests can join local fisherman Barker on his 'catch of the day' escapades when not enjoying the hotel's afternoon tea tradition or fantastic spa. Camelot's place as one of the island's top restaurants is ensured by Bajan chef Jason Joseph (an elegant white tablecloth affair). At the same time, monthly buffets and barbecues highlight local specialties in a more relaxed environment.

Address: Road View, Speightstown, Barbados (BB26025).

Price: Double rooms start at £307.

Club Coral Reef:

On The Coral Reef Club's lovely verandas, it's easy to envisage 20th-century writers composing chapters of sell-out novels. From the mahogany wicker armchairs softened with cream cushions to the ornate tea trays and heated doubles games before breakfast, the hotel exudes Old World elegance. Suites capitalize on this shamelessly classic yet laid-back motif, with gold-framed pictures reminiscent of an English country home, mahogany cabinets exhibiting coral, and those formal, structural sofas with soft cushions as rigid as they are. Guests can go along the boardwalk to beautiful Holetown (the first town founded on the island around 1695). However, the form here is usually poolside, with numerous rounds of rum cocktails.

The O'Hara family, who also own the Sandpiper and have been in Barbados since the 1950s, owns the hotel. As a result, despite the arrangement, in which two massive pools, a watersports area, and a spa appear to absorb the majority of the well-dressed crowd, a home-from-home vibe pervades. It's a huge draw, artfully weaved within acres of exquisite tropical vegetation as a massive open-air treatment complex. Guests float between first-class treatments and the thermal gardens or steam room, while yogis visit the relaxation room for bi-weekly yoga classes.

One premium restaurant relieves the agony of indecision by respectfully demanding a shirt and good manners.

Address: Porters Folkstone St. James, Barbados (BB24017).

Price: Double rooms start at £472.

Good Harbour, Little

There is an excellent, freewheeling alternative on the tranquil northwest coast, far from the jet set and dress code barbecue buffets. Little Good Harbour's whitewashed rooms are divided between the inland and seaside sides of the Coastal Road, with mild Bajan influences via local art and occasional splashes of color. Private kitchens and oversized marble baths make the suites feel more like private cottages than hotel rooms. Some have mahogany four-poster beds shrouded in mosquito nets, while others have large balconies with sophisticated sofas and armchairs to watch the sunset. The unifying thread is a relaxed and beautiful attitude.

The main coral stone structure shines onto a magnificent, slightly disheveled beach through green louvered shutters. From its lime-green porch, The Fish Pot enjoys the same vista; the restaurant has worked hard to capture the hearts (and stomachs) of locals and epicureans with a beautifully simple menu of fresh fish, pasta, and curries. It is now regarded as one of Barbados' most excellent restaurants, with no frills or exorbitant rates.

Guests can settle into green cushioned lounges beneath massive palms, sleep to the sound of flowing water from a Balinese sculpture, or (in the second, smaller pool) be surrounded by every shade of tropical green. A little spa packs a tremendous impact with a varied selection of massages and treatments. While cabin fever is unusual in this region, the lively Speightstown's modest shops, taverns, and cafés are only a five-minute drive away.

Address: Shermans, St. Lucy, Barbados

Price: Double rooms start at £250.

Beach at Sandy Lane

Sandy Lane, one of Barbados' most sumptuous hotels, sets an opulent tone with its polished marble flooring, old-fashioned armchairs framed by pot plants, and heart-wrenching sea views enclosed by stone arches and pillars. It backs onto a lovely stretch of blonde beach on the west coast, close to the vibrant Holetown. Despite the finest service, Neo-palladian stone guestrooms, and many diamonds glimmering under candlelight at supper, the ambiance is very laid-back.

After a leisurely buffet breakfast, guests can take golf buggies to one of Sandy Lane's three golf courses or spend the entire day in the palatial spa, which includes a sauna, steam room, and a hydrotherapy pool assault course, as well as an astonishing menu of delectable treatments ranging from Bajan sugar cane peels to Cryotherapy energy facials.

A gelato bar, watersports, and a very exceptional Treehouse Club for little children round out the country club idyll, allowing thankful parents to relax on the beach. The hotel's center point is a large layered pool with a waterfall, where sunbathers may see tennis whites or kaftans floating back from the bar with fresh Pia Coladas.

Address: Sandy Lane Hotel Sandy Lane, St. James, Barbados (BB24024).

Price: Double rooms start at £737.

The Sandpiper is a bird:

Despite its location on the busy edges of tourist-heavy Holetown, The Sandpiper shares the same easy-going elegance as its sister hotel, The Coral Reef Club (tucked a little north along the west coast). The golden sand and blue sea it backs upon are rarely empty, making for excellent people watching and following the movement of sailing boats and water skiers. Despite its small size, the hotel is surrounded by tropical gardens, with bougainvillea, palms, and ferns sprouting from every direction. Rooms alternate between a traditional, wicker-and-mahogany look and a more contemporary one, but all are vibrantly colored and printed.

An expansive sun terrace perched above the sand takes advantage of the ethereal beach vistas, especially at dusk when the sun burns a deep scarlet horizon. With rum cocktails in hand and deck shoes removed, guests enjoy the Sandpiper's laid-back vibe. The elegant open-air restaurant, surrounded by torch-lit tropical gardens, koi ponds, and delectable plates of Bajan flying fish, Caribbean shrimp, and lobster salads, calls for a linen shirt. While afternoons can be spent lounging by the large p and delicious magazine-worthy lap pool surrounded by alluring creamy parasols, the Coral Club's luxurious spa is just a concierge call away.

Address: Holetown, Barbados, 59Q6+CWP

Price: Double rooms start at £395.

Elegant Hotels' "The House":

The House, a modest and intimate hotel catering to adults only, adds a new dimension to Barbados' West Coast, usually home to more extensive and swankier hotels. With only 34 guestrooms, the atmosphere is hands-on and intimate. Check in and take your shoes off because you could stay at a friend's stylish beach house. Attentive hotel staff, dubbed "ambassadors," are on hand to provide homemade ice pops on the beach or to offer a gratis tour of Hunt's Gardens, a horticultural oasis constructed in the 1950s in the island's center.

The bedrooms are simple and elegant, from the cool terracotta floors to the enormous padded headboards. The sleek style is continued in the bathrooms, which have creamy marble vanities, rainfall showers, and full-sized, natural Elemental Herbology goods.

The House's substantial feature is its ability to stay wonderfully under the radar. For example, there is a complementary jet lag massage and a daily selection of wellness activities, such as Pilates and meditation sessions. The hotel is all-inclusive, but forget dull buffets; the offering is more fine-dining than 'fill-your-boots' grub. Positano's Champagne brunches, Afternoon tea in the Caribbean, and a crowd-pleasing coastal Italian menu are genuinely sophisticated. At the same time, nightcaps at the 1703 Mount Gay Rum Bar are a fun-fueled way to end the day Bajan-style. The following day, you can unwind by floating in the tranquil waters at Paynes Bay Beach, which is known as the best area on the island to bathe.

Address: Elegant Hotels, Paynes Bay, St. James, Barbados, BB24023

Price: Double rooms start at £807 per night.

Tamarind:

Tamarind, Elegant Hotels' Barbados portfolio's most family-friendly hotel, is ideal for children and teens. Swimming is safe for small children in the crystal clear waters of Paynes Bay while kayaking, sailing, and snorkeling can keep larger children entertained for hours. Children can also participate in a dedicated island experience, where they will learn local words, prepare traditional Bajan cuisine, and receive a Bajan "passport."

The 101 bedrooms are bright and breezy, with splashes of color from modern artwork, rugs, and colorful linens. For dining, look for Bajan specialties like flying fish, roti, and macaroni pie, or use the 'Dine Around' program to visit other Elegant Resorts resorts for a change of scenery.

Tamarind's days begin with fresh papaya juice, traditional 'bakes,' and the fluffiest herb omelets. Go snorkeling at the beach, where you might see marine turtles and manta rays, or to one of the three pools, where you can chill off with fruit kebabs and ice cream.

Address: Paynes Bay, Barbados, BB24023 Tamarind by Elegant Hotels

Price: Double rooms start at £520.

CHAPTER FOUR: ATTRACTIONS AND SIGHTSEEING

Beaches and Natural Wonders

Barbados is well-known for its beautiful beaches, each with its distinct personality. The island's shoreline offers a variety of experiences, from the legendary golden sands of the west coast to the more rugged, surf-friendly coastlines of the east. Crane Beach, noted for its pink beaches and towering cliffs, and Bathsheba Beach, a favorite among surfers for its big waves and spectacular rock formations, are two highlights. The west coast's tranquil, turquoise waters, such as those in Payne's Bay, are great for swimming and snorkeling, with beautiful coral reefs teeming with marine life. Exploring the coastal wonders also includes discovering hidden coves, sampling beachfront cuisine, and participating in water sports like jet skiing and paddleboarding.

Historical Monuments and Museums

Barbados' rich past is highlighted by its numerous historical sites and museums. Bridgetown, the country's capital, is a UNESCO World Heritage site. They contain colonial architecture and historic structures like the Parliament Buildings and the Garrison. The Barbados Museum and Historical Society tells the island's story, from its indigenous beginnings to colonial and modern times. Plantation houses such as St. Nicholas Abbey and Sunbury Plantation House provide insight into the island's history as a sugar plantation. Culturally noteworthy sites include the George Washington House, where the future American president stayed, and the Nidhe Israel Synagogue, one of the Western Hemisphere's oldest synagogues.

Natural Attractions and Parks

In addition to its beaches, Barbados has several natural attractions and parks that exhibit its biodiversity and natural beauty. Harrison's Cave is an extraordinary crystalline limestone cavern with flowing streams and huge ponds. The tropical forest of Welchman Hall Gully allows visitors to witness natural flora and fauna, including the island's green monkeys. The Flower Forest and Hunte's

Gardens are botany fans' dream destinations, with beautiful landscapes filled with exotic plants and flowers. The Barbados Wildlife Reserve is a shelter for various species, including deer, peacocks, and iguanas, where animals can move freely in their natural habitat.

Cultural and Community Activities

Barbados' calendar is jam-packed with cultural and community events representing the island's rich history and lively modern culture. The Crop Over Festival evolved from colonial-era harvest celebrations to a stunning exhibition of song, dance, and extravagant costumes, culminating in the Grand Kadooment Day parade. Parades, cultural displays, and the lighting of Bridgetown in national colors are all part of the Independence Day celebrations. The Holetown Festival honors Barbados' earliest English colony with a history, culture, and entertainment week. Regular fish fries at Oistins and Speightstown, where locals and visitors enjoy freshly caught seafood, music, and dancing, are iconic Bajan experiences that create community spirit and highlight local traditions.

These summaries serve as a starting point for a more in-depth examination of the issues. To meet the word count requirement, each section can be enlarged by providing more precise details, personal anecdotes, interviews with locals or experts, and a more extensive discussion of the importance of these factors to Barbados' identity and tourism.

Top 10 destinations to explore in Barbados

1. The capital city of Bridgetown

One of the most famous places in Barbados, Bridgetown is the central city and the most developed port in the Caribbean. When British colonists landed on the island in 1628, only a wooden bridge and a local tribe of Arawaks were found on the modern city's site. Later, the village of St. Michael was established and rapidly developed through the trade of foreign settlers. The town received its current name, "Bridgetown," much later, after centuries.

Like most tourist cities around the world, Bridgetown is a place of strong contrasts - a simple walk through the center of the city can open many sides of urban life: rusty bikes, electric bikes, supercars, ancient cars of the 70's - things that captivate the eye in the first place.

There is a picturesque National Heroes Square in the heart of one of the best places to visit in Barbados, decorated with fountains and monuments, including Admiral Nelson. And in a few blocks, you can find the parish church of St. James - its interior decoration has not changed much over the centuries. Bridgetown contains many places to visit in Barbados - cultural monuments and iconic historical sites, some of which we will consider in more detail below.

2. George Washington House

This historic structure was known as the Bush Hill House in the 18th century and was home to plantations where crops were cultivated. In 1751, a young man named George Washington and his half-brother Lawrence from the United States spent two months in Barbados. Later, this young man would become his country's first president, and Barbados was his lone foreign visit. For many years, the property remained closed and useless (until 1999) until the Barbados National Foundation decided to restore the building and turn it into a historic-cultural monument. George Washington House, one of the finest attractions in Barbados, reopened to the public in January 2007 after undergoing extensive repair. The operating hours are daily from 9:00 to 16:30 local time, the Monday through Friday admittance fee totals around $25.

Address: Bush Hill, The Garrison, St. Michael, Barbados.

3. Crane Beach and The Crane Resort

With its pink coral sand, Crane Beach was once a boat station surrounded by rocks. Now, it's one of the best beaches in Barbados. Tourists and locals come here to enjoy surfing, sunbathing on sun loungers, and stop by the luxurious The Crane overlooking the water and sand.

The Crane Resort is the oldest hotel in the Caribbean and has operated since 1887. It is enormous: it has 252 rooms, five large swimming pools, five restaurants and bars, a wide area with an art gallery, and numerous amenities scattered throughout the region. The elegant colonial-style rooms have kitchenettes, private swimming pools, Jacuzzis, and small gymnasiums.

The resort is located on the main road in the eastern part of the island. The area is clean and well-maintained, with palm trees, tropical greenery, winding paths, and small bridges. The central buildings are large and painted in neutral beige with towers on the sides. This one of the famous places in Barbados looks more like a charming old town with colorful structures, ancient entrances, and carved window overhangs than a hotel.

Resort address: The Crane Resort, St. Philip, Barbados.

4. St. Nicholas Abbey

The next one in our top 10 places to visit in Barbados is St. Nicholas Abbey. The Danish-style building spans three stories and formerly served as the central hub of a vast sugar cane plantation and a little oil refinery. Founded in 1650, the abbey was the private residence of a certain Colonel Beringer, who completed his earthly journey during a duel. A beautiful legend says that the colonel's immortal soul is still wandering the corridors of an old building.Despite its religious name, the abbey is considered an utterly secular and privately owned building. Only the ground floor of the building is always open to tourists.

The main things that catch the eye at the entrance are: The fireplaces with the original coral finish.

- High balls of carved stone.
- Corner chimneys.

In a souvenir shop near this, one of the best places to visit in Barbados, you can buy real pirate rum from the local cane sugar plantation.

Address: St Nicholas Abbey, Cherry Tree Hill, St Peter, BB 26007, Barbados.

5. Folkestone Marine Park and Museum

Folkestone Marine Park is in Holetown, near St. James' Parish Church. It boasts an artificial reef formed by the wreck of the Stavronikita, about half a kilometer from the shore. The ship now serves as a landmark in Barbados and as home to much marine life: lilies, corals, sea sponges, and numerous small fish. Diving in the Marine Park is allowed only for experienced divers - the waters are sometimes calm, and the depths are considerable. Usually, tourists are offered safe tours on a boat with a clear glass bottom: sea flora and fauna open as "in the palm of his hand," and the shipwreck is perfectly visible.

The center of one of the interesting Barbados attractions - Folkestone Museum- is a massive aquarium with sporadic forms of marine life - an educational place for adults and tourists with children.

Address: Church Point, Holetown, St. James, Barbados.

6. Harrison's Cave

It is a unique natural attraction in Barbados and is listed by locals as one of the "7 Wonders of the Island". It opens a beautiful world of stalactites and stalagmites, clear waters, the oldest emerald lakes, and small waterfalls. Nowadays, Harrison's Cave is a renowned tourist destination on the mysterious island and around the Caribbean. Harrison's Cave was discovered in the 18th century but was explored in the 1970s. After four years, it became a full-fledged tourist attraction of Barbados, freely open to all comers.

The length of the Harrison cave is about 2.3 km. The underground world has more than 50 "separate rooms" connected by natural tunnels.

The largest hall is more than 30 meters high. On the cave expanses, sometimes animals are found: bats, green monkeys, and small fish in lakes. Tourists can visit the underground complex daily, except on state holidays. The cave zone has a bar, a restaurant, and tents for shopping with souvenirs.

Address: Welchman Hall, Saint Thomas, Allen View, Barbados.

7. Morgan Lewis Windmill

The Morgan Lewis Windmill was constructed in 1727 in the northern part of St. Andrew, situated along the island's eastern coastline, in close proximity to the sole surviving sugar mill on the island. The mill is ranked fourth among the "7 Wonders of the Island." In 1999, a complete restoration was carried out at about 800,000 USD. The Barbados National Foundation protects this historical monument and displays equipment powered by nature's "clean energy." Reed juice for tasting is available for everyone.

The Morgana Lewis Windmill is the only functioning windmill in the world that grinds sugar cane and is one of our planet's 100 most protected landmarks.

Address: Morgan Lewis Windmill, St. Andrew, Barbados.

8. Emancipation Statue

The Statue of Emancipation is one of the must-see places to visit in Barbados. The Emancipation Statue is an iconic Barbados landmark created by Karl Broodhagen, the island's most prominent sculptor and architect. In literal translation, the sculpture symbolizes the "breaking of the chains of slavery." The subjects were liberated entirely in 1838, with over 70,000 native and African Barbadoses throwing their iron fetters and triumphing through the streets of the free kingdom. The second name of the Emancipation Statue was "Bussa," the name of the enslaved West African who led the first rebellion for involuntary rights and freedom in 1816.

Bussa is now on the list of national heroes in Barbados despite its origins in the Black Continent.

Address: Bridgetown, Emancipation Statue (Bussa Statue), Barbados.

9. Carlisle Bay

The Carlisle Bay is a natural harbor and bay in the shape of an elongated arc on the west coast of Barbados, which gently "flows" into Bridgetown's port. It is often "anchored" by luxury boats, yachts, and other seagoing ships and boats. The Carlisle is perfect for all kinds of water sports and diving - the harbor is usually calm, and the underwater world's diversity has been striking for a long time.

Beaches of the bay: Brandon's Beach, Pebbles Beach, and Beishore Beach. They are about 3 kilometers southwest of Bridgetown city center. Free parking, lifeguards, toilets, and shops are available throughout the property. The entrance is free, and all beaches are open from sunrise to sunset on any day of the week.

10.   Bathsheba

The quaint village of Bathsheba is considered to be the center of Barbados's attractions for tourists on the island's east coast. The botanical gardens "Andromeda" and "Flower Forest" are nearby. On the beach of Bathsheba, also known as the "Soup Bowl," large rock formations (remains of an ancient coral reef) from afar resemble "giant mushrooms" growing directly from the sea. This is one of the best beaches in Barbados and is excellent for filming and surfing, but strong currents can be dangerous - you should always be careful not to take risks in vain.

If you want to hide from the crowds and escape nature, Atlantis Hotel and the Sea-U Guest House, located next to the rocky beach, will help you.

CHAPTER 5: ACTIVITIES AND EXPERIENCES

Water Sports and Marine Adventures

Barbados is an island in the eastern Caribbean. It is a water sports and marine adventurer's paradise. With its crystal-clear seas, vivid coral reefs, and wealth of marine life, the island provides a wide selection of activities for all skill levels and interests, from tranquil snorkeling to adrenaline-pumping kite surfing.

Windsurfing and surfing

Barbados is a well-known surfing destination around the world. The Soup Bowl at Bathsheba, the island's most famous surf break, is recognized for its consistent, powerful waves that draw surfers worldwide. Bathsheba's rough, pristine beauty and tough leaves make it a surfer's heaven. With its robust and constant trade winds and warm, turquoise waters, Silver Sands on the south coast is great for windsurfing and kite surfing.

Silver Sands is a fantastic site for beginners and specialists to learn or hone their talents, with several local schools offering courses and equipment.

Snorkeling and Scuba Diving

Barbados' undersea life is equally as appealing as the island's surface. The island's west shore, with its calm, clear seas, is ideal for snorkeling. Snorkelers can swim with Hawksbill and Green turtles here, a genuinely magical experience. Carlisle Bay, a marine park, is a popular snorkeling and diving destination. This area is home to multiple shipwrecks teaming with marine life and has created artificial reefs that are a refuge for divers. Scuba diving expeditions to deeper seas reveal larger species, such as barracudas and reef sharks, for the more daring.

Kayaking and stand-up paddleboarding

SUP and kayaking are becoming increasingly popular in Barbados, providing a more leisurely approach to appreciate the Island's picturesque shoreline. Paddleboarding, in particular, is a terrific opportunity to explore the West

Coast's quiet, crystal-clear waters, providing a unique perspective of the island's marine life. Many resorts and coastal businesses hire paddle boards and kayaks, and guided trips are offered for those interested in exploring specific areas.

Deep Sea Fishing

For those searching for a more adventurous marine adventure, deep-sea fishing off the coast of Barbados is an excellent option. Because of the island's location in the Atlantic, there are plenty of large game fish, including marlin, tuna, and wahoo. It is expected to charter a boat for a day of deep-sea fishing, with expert captains guiding anglers to the best spots.

Barbados is a destination that offers outstanding water activities and marine adventures. Whether you're a surfer looking for the perfect wave, a diver exploring the depths, or a fisherman looking for the big catch, Barbados has it all. Due to space limitations, I can only present a thorough examination of one issue at a time. Please let me know if you want to go on to the next topic, "Hiking and Outdoor Activities," or any other subtopic!

CHAPTER 6: FOOD AND DINING

Traditional Bajan Cuisine

The Essence of Barbadian Flavors: A Journey Through Traditional Bajan Cuisine

Barbadian cuisine, also called Bajan cuisine, is an excellent expression of the island's rich cultural tapestry weaved through centuries of history. Influenced by West African, British, Indian, and Creole traditions, the culinary environment of Barbados is a diverse blend of flavors, spices, and techniques.

Historical Roots and Influences

The story of Bajan cuisine is a chronicle of the island's history. From the indigenous Arawaks and Caribs, who introduced Barbados to cassava and sweet potatoes, to the enslaved Africans who brought okra and plantains, each wave of occupants left an unmistakable stamp on the island's culinary customs. The British colonial period introduced cured meats and puddings, adding another layer to this rich mosaic.

Staple Ingredients and Classic Dishes

The core of Bajan cookery rests in utilizing fresh, local ingredients. The extensive marine life surrounding the island makes seafood a significant diet component. The national dish of Barbados, flying fish served with cou-cou (made from cornmeal and okra), embodies the essence of the island's flavors. Another staple is Bajan seasoning, a blend of herbs and spices including thyme, marjoram, and scotch bonnet peppers that marinade meats and shellfish, imparting a distinct Caribbean flavor.

Pudding and souse, a traditional Saturday dish, displays the island's inventiveness. Made with sweet potato pudding and pickled pig, it's a testament to the confluence of African and British cultures. Meanwhile, fish cakes, a famous street meal, are an excellent snack prepared from salted cod combined with herbs and spices, deep-fried to golden perfection.

Cooking Techniques

Bajan cooking techniques are basic yet effective, emphasizing the products' natural flavors. Grilling over an open flame, known as grilling, is a favored approach, especially for fish. Slow-cooking stews and soups, like the renowned Bajan Pepper Pot, a hearty stew of meat and vegetables, allow for a natural merging of tastes.

Cultural Significance

Food in Barbados is more than nourishment; it's a form of expression and a source of pride. Traditional meals generally relate to specific holidays and celebrations, emphasizing their cultural significance. For instance, cookies and steamed cornmeal cakes blended with pumpkin, coconut, and spices are usually produced for Independence Day celebrations.

Beverages: From Mauby to Rum

All investigation of Bajan cuisine is complete with mentioning its drinks. Mauby, a beverage prepared from the bark of the Colubrina tree, is a local favorite recognized for its peculiar, somewhat bitter taste. And then there's rum, a vital aspect of Barbadian heritage. Distilled from sugarcane, Barbadian rum is renowned worldwide, frequently drunk neat or in drinks like the famed Rum Punch.

Modern Interpretations

Traditional Bajan cuisine has recently seen a resurgence, with chefs reinterpreting them with new touches. These contemporary interpretations honor the spirit of the conventional while incorporating new flavors and presentation approaches, making Bajan cuisine appealing to a worldwide palate. Traditional Bajan food is a delectable trip through the island's history and culture. Each dish tells a narrative, and each flavor is unique. Sings a song of the past and present, making Barbadian cuisine more than just a culinary delight but a rich cultural experience.

This essay gives an in-depth look at traditional Bajan cuisine, reflecting its essence and significance. For thorough reports on "Fine Dining and International Cuisine" and "Street Food and Casual Eats," further comments would be necessary. Please let me know whether you would like to proceed with either of these topics!

Fine Dining & International Cuisine:

Barbados' fine dining scene is diversified and dynamic, making it a culinary destination for visitors seeking great foreign food. There are numerous high-end eateries on the island, each with its distinct flavor profile. The Cliff, famed for its stunning beachside setting and combination of Caribbean and Mediterranean flavors, is a prime example of Barbadian gourmet dining. Champers is another renowned restaurant with an extensive wine selection and a menu that includes lobster and grilled seafood. International cuisine is also available, from Japanese sushi at Nishi to Italian specialties at Cin Cin By The Sea. Barbados' fine dining experiences are famed for their exceptional service and breathtaking vistas, making them ideal for special occasions.

Street Food and Fast Food:

While Barbados excels in sophisticated dining, the vibrant world of street food and casual eats is equally celebrated. Roadside vendors and local markets provide a variety of delectable selections that highlight the island's distinct flavors. The distinctive "cutters," which are sandwiches stuffed with local ingredients like flying fish, cou-cou, and hot Bajan pepper sauce, are a must-try for visitors. Roti, a Caribbean flatbread packed with curried chicken, beef, or veggies, is frequently served by food trucks and kiosks. Try the fish fry-ups at Oistins Fish Market for a genuinely Bajan experience, where you can eat freshly caught fish, macaroni pie, and coleslaw while listening to live music and enjoying a lively atmosphere. Barbados' street cuisine and informal eats offer a compelling and economical way to taste the island's gastronomic delights, whether at a street cart, rum shop, or beachside shack.

Fine Dining & International Cuisine:

Barbados' fine dining scene is diversified and dynamic, making it a culinary destination for visitors seeking great foreign food. There are numerous high-end eateries on the island, each with its distinct flavor profile. The Cliff, famed for its stunning beachside setting and combination of Caribbean and Mediterranean flavors, is a prime example of Barbadian gourmet dining. Champers is another renowned restaurant with an extensive wine selection and a menu that includes lobster and grilled seafood. International cuisine is also available, from Japanese sushi at Nishi to Italian specialties at Cin Cin By The Sea. Barbados' fine dining experiences are famed for their exceptional service and breathtaking vistas, making them ideal for special occasions.

Street Food and Fast Food:

While Barbados excels in sophisticated dining, the vibrant world of street food and casual eats is equally celebrated. Roadside vendors and local markets provide a variety of delectable selections that highlight the island's distinct flavors. The distinctive "cutters," which are sandwiches stuffed with local ingredients like flying fish, cou-cou, and hot Bajan pepper sauce, are a must-try for visitors. Roti, a Caribbean flatbread packed with curried chicken, beef, or veggies, is frequently served by food trucks and kiosks. Try the fish fry-ups at Oistins Fish Market for a genuinely Bajan experience, where you can eat freshly caught fish, macaroni pie, and coleslaw while listening to live music and enjoying a lively atmosphere. Barbados' street cuisine and informal eats offer a compelling and economical way to taste the island's gastronomic delights, whether at a street cart, rum shop, or beachside shack.

CHAPTER 7: PRACTICAL INFORMATION FOR TRAVELERS

Health and Safety Recommendations

Barbados is no exception when it comes to health and safety. To ensure a safe and pleasurable vacation, be aware of the following health and safety tips:

Vaccinations and Health Precautions:

Consult a healthcare provider before flying to Barbados to ensure you are currently on routine immunizations. Depending on your schedule and personal health history, extra vaccinations or preventive measures, such as those for Hepatitis A and B or typhoid, may be recommended.

Water and Food Safety:

Barbados' tap water is typically safe to drink, but bottled water may be preferable if you have a sensitive stomach.

To limit the danger of foodborne diseases while dining out, stick to well-known restaurants and cafés.

Sun protection:

Barbados has a tropical environment with an abundance of sunshine. Use high-SPF sunscreen, sunglasses, and a wide-brimmed hat to avoid sunburn. To prevent heat-related illnesses, stay hydrated throughout the day.

Mosquito-Borne Diseases:

While there isn't a high risk of mosquito-borne diseases in Barbados, using insect repellent is still a good idea, especially in the evening.
Consider staying at a hotel that has mosquito nets or window screens.

Beach Safety:

Barbados has lovely beaches, although some spots may have violent currents and undertows. At beaches, pay heed to warning flags and signs.

If you are not a strong swimmer, consider visiting beaches where lifeguards are on duty.

COVID-19 Precautions:

COVID-19 protections may still be in place as of my last knowledge update in January 2022. Check your government's and Barbados' current travel advisories and health guidelines. As needed, follow mask-wearing and social separation norms.

Cultural Etiquette and Customs

Understanding and appreciating Barbados' local culture and customs can improve your vacation experience and help you engage with the locals successfully:

Dress code:

Barbados has a relaxed dress code, especially along the coast. However, dress modestly and conservatively when visiting churches or premium restaurants or attending formal occasions.

Greetings and politeness:

Barbadians are generally polite and friendly. When meeting someone for the first time, a simple "Good morning" or "Good afternoon" is usual.
Use "sir" or "ma'am" to show respect when addressing elders.

Punctuality:

Barbadians have a laid-back attitude toward time, but being on time for business meetings and formal events is essential.

Dining Etiquette:

When dining with natives, waiting until the host initiates the meal is customary. Try foods like "flying fish and cou-cou" or "pepperpot."

Traditions should be respected:

Barbados has a diverse cultural background. Respect local traditions and practices, such as the Crop Over Festival or other cultural festivals.

Photographic Etiquette:

Always seek permission before photographing people or their property. Some people may choose not to be photographed.

Communication and connectivity

Staying connected and communicating effectively in Barbados is critical for a good trip. Here are several communication and connectivity pointers:

Language:

Because English is the official language of Barbados, most inhabitants are conversant in it. You should have no issue conversing in English.

Mobile Network and Internet:

Barbados has a well-developed mobile network, and you may use your phone with a local SIM card to access data and make local calls.

Connecting is simple because many hotels, restaurants, and cafes offer free Wi-Fi.

Emergency Services:

In Barbados, dial 911 for police, medical, or fire emergencies.

Currency and Payments:

Barbados accepts the Barbadian dollar (BBD), while the US currency is frequently welcomed. Credit cards are also often used for payment.

Postal Services:

The postal service in Barbados is dependable, and you can mail postcards or letters from local post offices.

Time Zone:

Throughout the year, Barbados adheres to Eastern Standard Time (EST), GMT-4. You can have a more comfortable and gratifying experience in Barbados if you remember these health and safety considerations, cultural etiquette, and communication standards. Always stay current on the most recent travel advisories and local rules to guarantee a safe and comfortable journey.

CHAPTER 8: DAY TRIPS AND EXCURSIONS

Attractions and Islands Nearby

Barbados is a terrific destination in its own right, with its magnificent beaches, vibrant culture, and rich history. It is, nevertheless, a gateway to several adjacent islands and sights worth visiting:

Grenadines:

The Grenadines are a beautiful line of islands and cays easily accessible from Barbados. Bequia, Mustique, and Tobago Cays are all must-see islands. These islands are known for their crystal-clear waters, great diving, and private resorts.

Saint Lucia:

Another Caribbean jewel, St. Lucia, is only a short flight from Barbados. Visitors can explore the renowned Pitons, relax on lovely beaches, and visit Sulphur Springs. St. Lucia also has jungle hiking and adventure activities available.

Martinique:

Martinique is a French-speaking island famous for its French-Caribbean culture, lush scenery, and historical sites. Explore Fort-de-France, hike Mont Pelée, and eat excellent Creole food.

10.1.4 Saint Vincent:

The nearby island of St. Vincent has volcanic landscapes, waterfalls, and black-sand beaches. Hiking at the La Soufrière volcano and exploring Wallilabou Bay, a filming location for the "Pirates of the Caribbean" films, are available on the island.

Historical Sites:

Barbados' historical sites include St. Nicholas Abbey, George Washington House, and Bridgetown's UNESCO-listed Garrison Historic Area. These sites shed light on the island's colonial history.

Wildlife & Nature Reserves:

Barbados has ecological reserves that showcase the island's unique flora and fauna, such as the Barbados Wildlife Reserve and the Andromeda Botanic Gardens. Exploring these reserves is an excellent opportunity to get in touch with nature.

Tours and Activities Planned

Barbados has various excursions and activities that suit different interests. There is something for everyone, whether you are an explorer, a history buff, or someone who appreciates leisure activities:

Island Tours:

Take a guided island trip to see the highlights of Barbados, such as the rocky east coast, ancient buildings, and lovely fishing villages. Tours frequently include stops at Bathsheba, Hunte's Gardens, and St. John's Parish Church.

Catamaran Cruises:

Catamaran cruises are a popular method of seeing the Caribbean Sea's splendor. These tours frequently involve snorkeling, swimming with sea turtles, and a great lunch served onboard.

Tours of Rum Distilleries:

Barbados is famous for its rum, and rum fans should visit one of the island's ancient distilleries, such as Mount Gay or Foursquare. Discover the rum-making process and taste some of the finest spirits.

Wildlife Encounters:

Participate in nature trips to see sea turtles breeding or hatching on the beaches. These visits provide a once-in-a-lifetime opportunity to witness the conservation efforts underway to safeguard these endangered species.

Plantation Tours:

Tour St. Nicholas Abbey or Sunbury Plantation House to learn about the island's sugar plantation heritage. These trips offer insight into Barbados' colonial history.

Itineraries for Self-Guided Travel

Self-guided tours allow you to discover Barbados at your speed, which is ideal for those who prefer a more independent experience. Here are some self-guided recommendations:

Beachcombing:

Barbados has many gorgeous beaches. Make your beach-hopping plan, beginning with popular destinations such as Crane Beach, Accra Beach, and Carlisle Bay.

Bridgetown's Historic District:

Bridgetown's old capital city can be explored on foot. Visit historic sites such as Independence Square, the Parliament Buildings, and the Nidhe Israel Synagogue.

Culinary Tour:

Try local dishes at numerous eateries and food booths for a culinary experience. Take advantage of the chance to try flying fish, cou-cou, and fish cakes.

CHAPTER 9
SUSTAINABLE TOURISM IN BARBADOS

Environmental Initiatives

Like many other tourist locations, Barbados is dedicated to protecting its natural environment and solving environmental issues. Travelers can help these efforts and lessen their ecological imprint by being environmentally conscious and participating in a variety of initiatives:

Beach Cleanups:

Many local organizations and hotels organize beach cleanup events. These efforts contribute to the preservation of Barbados' beautiful beaches and the protection of marine life.

Marine Conservation:

Barbados is home to several marine conservation groups, including the Barbados Sea Turtle Project. Travelers can contribute to these projects by making a gift or participating in guided turtle-watching trips, promoting respectful engagement with sea turtles.

Long-Term Accommodations:

Choose eco-friendly lodging that follows sustainable methods. Look for hotels and resorts with certifications, such as Green Globe or EarthCheck, demonstrating their dedication to environmental sustainability.

Waste Management:

Bring reusable water bottles, shopping bags, and utensils to reduce plastic waste. Many Barbadian companies are taking steps to reduce their use of single-use plastics.

Transportation Sustainability:

To reduce carbon emissions when exploring the island, choose eco-friendly transportation choices such as electric buses or carpooling.

Contribute to Local Conservation Projects:

Donations or volunteer opportunities might be used to support local environmental efforts. The Barbados National Trust works to conserve the island's natural heritage.

Assistance to Local Communities

Barbados is more than simply beaches and resorts; it also has a thriving local culture and villages. Travelers may help these communities in a variety of ways, including:

Buy Local:

Souvenirs and products can be purchased from local craftspeople, marketplaces, and businesses. You are directly supporting the livelihoods of local entrepreneurs and artisans by doing so.

Eat at a Local Restaurant:

At local eateries and restaurants, you may sample traditional Bajan cuisine. This supports local businesses and encourages cultural interchange.

Accommodations in Boutiques:

Consider staying at a tiny, independently owned boutique hotel or guesthouse. This benefits the local economy and allows you to experience genuine Bajan hospitality.

Participate in Local Communities

Participate in community-based tourist activities such as guided neighborhood tours or cultural festivals. This helps residents gain a better grasp of Barbadian culture.

Volunteer:

Consider volunteering with local organizations focusing on education, healthcare, or community development if you have the time and talent. Volunteering is an effective way to give back to the community.

Observe Local Customs:

Learn about and appreciate Barbados' cultural norms and practices. Simple gestures like welcome and polite behavior can go a long way toward fostering favorable relationships with locals.

Tips for Safe Travel

Responsible travel entails making thoughtful decisions to reduce your environmental effects, respect local customs, and positively contribute to the areas you visit. Here are some sensible travel suggestions for Barbados:

Reduce Your Use of Plastic:

Barbados has taken initiatives to prevent plastic trash, and visitors may help by reducing their usage of single-use plastics. Bring your reusable water bottle and shopping bag, and avoid using plastic straws.

Water and energy conservation:

In your accommodations, conserve water and electricity. When not in use, reuse towels and switch off lights and air conditioning.

Selecting Sustainable Tours:

Look for tour providers who stress sustainability and ethical tourism practices when scheduling tours and excursions. Inquire about their community and environmental activities.

Contribute to Wildlife Conservation:

If you engage in wildlife-related activities, ensure they are ethical and do not injure or exploit animals. Look for tour companies who are committed to responsible wildlife tourism.

Protected areas must be respected:

When visiting natural reserves and protected places, adhere to the rules and regulations. Avoid upsetting wildlife by staying on authorized trails.

Reduce Water Consumption:

Water might be scarce in Barbados, so use it wisely throughout your visit. Inform your lodging of any leakage or wasteful activities.

Discover Local Culture:

Consider learning about Barbadian culture, history, and customs. This will improve your trip experience and allow you to interact more appropriately with locals.

Snorkeling and diving should be done responsibly:

Avoid harming or injuring coral reefs and marine life if you enjoy snorkeling or diving. To safeguard fragile underwater habitats, use reef-safe sunscreen. You may have a good impact on Barbados by following these environmental efforts, supporting local communities, and following responsible travel tips. Reliable tourism benefits the destination and enhances your trip experience by encouraging meaningful connections and cultural knowledge.

CONCLUSION

As our voyage through the gorgeous island of Barbados comes to an end, it's difficult not to feel a strong connection to this vibrant land and its warm people. Barbados, a jewel in the Caribbean's crown, is a feeling, an experience that lingers in the heart long after the sandy footprints are washed away.

We've traveled throughout a region rich in culture, heritage, and natural beauty, from the sun-drenched beaches of the Platinum Coast to the historic streets of Bridgetown. We danced to calypso rhythms, experienced the hot tastes of Bajan food, and felt the warmth of the Bajan spirit in every grin and greeting.

The splendor of the island extends beyond its beautiful beaches and into the lush, green heartlands, where sugar cane fields sway and tropical flowers flourish. The rough east coast of Barbados, with its spectacular cliffs and pounding surf, has shown us a distinct, harsher side of the island, reminding us of the many landscapes that this little island covers. As visitors, we've had the luxury of witnessing the island's dedication to protecting its natural and cultural riches. Barbados is a place where the past and current coexist seamlessly, from conservation work in the Graeme Hall Nature Sanctuary to the restoration of old Bridgetown and its Garrison.

Barbados' true treasure, however, is its people. With their unwavering warmth and contagious zeal for life, the Bajans have made our tour unforgettable. Their stories, humor, and traditions are the spirit of the island, drawing us back again and again.As you end this travel guide, keep in mind that Barbados is more than simply a destination; it is an experience that becomes a part of you. Whether you're visiting for the first time or returning to familiar territory, the island's magic, beauty, and warmth linger, inviting you back to its sunlit beaches and colorful culture.

Until we meet again, Barbados, stay sparkling like the Caribbean jewel that you are.

Printed in Great Britain
by Amazon